UIL

W0017079

N6
EL 7017

The Border

Katlyn

The Border

Cleatus Rattan

—Winner, 2002 Texas Review Poetry Prize—

Texas Review Press
Huntsville, Texas

Copyright © 2002 by Cleatus Rattan
All rights reserved
Printed in the United States of America

FIRST EDITION, 2002

Requests for permission to reproduce material from this work should be sent to:

>   Permissions
>   *Texas Review* Press
>   English Department
>   Sam Houston State University
>   Huntsville, TX 77341-2146

Grateful acknowledgment to the following journals and anthologies, in which many of these poems, some in slightly altered form, have appeared: *Concho River Review, Descant, New Texas (91, 92, 98, 99, 00, 01), Red Owl, RE Arts & Letters, Sands, Sanscrit, TEX!, Texas Anthology, Texas Review, Windhover, Wormwood Review, Yearbook of American Poetry—1985*. Several poems also appeared in the chapbooks *The Red Lion* and *130 Miles to Dallas*.

Cover design by Paul Ruffin

Cover photograph by Cathi Ball

Library of Congress Cataloging-in-Publication Data

Rattan, Cleatus, 1935-
      The Border / Cleatus Rattan.-- 1st ed.
         p. cm.
      ISBN 1-881515-47-8 (alk. paper)
         1. Mexican American Border Region--Poetry. 2. Texas, West--Poetry.
   I. Title

   PS3618.A88 B67 2002
   811'.6--dc21
                                                                2002005248

For Connie

Contents

Reading Hometown Obituaries

She looked like Judy's good witch, Billie Burke,
whose silver wand waved a floating caress.

With not so much a hurried push or ram
as a sliding wiggle, I could squirm
through, after Sunday double feature matinees,
almost to the front of blinding, mirrored light
where Judy Fey buried her hand right
in the sure and holy depth of all goodness.
With her cap a laurel, a halo in florescent rays,
she lifted almost all young distresses,
scooping high from a bin of hard pure white.

I confirm I remain a vanilla-loving man.

My eyes, transfixed, worshipped at her short sleeves,
as she extracted creamy fingers, knuckles.
I feared an empty, wicked spell—a drought
before my flattened nose. She rapidly circled
above her container-demense, a diurnal breeze,
cyclonic even, asking, "Single dip or double?"
In heat before conditioned air, no doubt
two scoops could drip to elbow trouble,
but who worth a dime could say, "Single, please?"

Even though your enchantments could turn to mess,
I pray you may remain in bewitching goodness,
loving, lovely Judy Mary Fey Lauck,
whose sweet caress could shame the actress Billie Burke.

Cynthia's Relection

I turn out the small lamp
beside my bed and walk
to the window to see the light
drawn out and up. But I know
the moon gathers my energy
to spread on lovers like my son
who, two hundred miles from home
at my old college, is at this moment,
I hope, in his car with some young lovely
who reminds me of his mother
now breathing softly, waiting
for me to come to her
before all our light is gone.

Screen Saver

In twenty seconds the computer builds
then disposes of intricate patterns.
(My bald spot grows at about the same speed.)
But beautiful figures which I would keep
disappear into some unknown terminal
while the world travels toward some black hole,
no known direction, to the gray in my eyebrows,
which hover above me until I dissolve.
I dissolve. My wife, eating ice cream,
stands behind me, smiles, pats my head.

Morning Rituals

I saddle my horse in darkness and ride north
to the lake, looking for new calves. I must know
no golden hereford has slipped into greener
fields. She opens the French doors to the patio
and sees green and blue water of the pool.
Her eyes reflect the liquid as she sees a touch
of morning moisture on a red-wood table
holding amber juice and dark toast.
Her golden, layered hair ripples gently
in the wind like clouds flowing opposite
directions at different heights. Brown leaves
in the pool blow back and forth,
growing larger, smaller, floating beneath
rising mist. My big bay horse, impatient
to return, stabs the lake edge with his hoof,
shakes his body to say that we have looked
enough at murky reflections. She opens
yesterday's paper, uninterested in daily things.
A big bronze cat catches her eye
as it climbs the fence, eager for the barn.
I scan the north mountains
that roll in thunder. She steps back
in the house to wake our sons
for school. I turn south,
eager to learn her flesh again.

A Popular Play

Only a few seconds left and I, third rate
actor, was sent in to the stage
where I was not the primary lamb.

Teiresias saw it all so clearly, the message
came to me. Too proud to know, I flicked
my hands up in lights and pulled it snugly

to my chest, certain of destiny. Deftly out
then in and a would be hero fell, groping
for me, no hand upon him. Breathing deeply,

already inflated as the globe, I saw Achilles
come to conflict through the last
Hector. Tantalizing him, sure of Athena,

I came close, picked up speed Hermes envied
and cut at an angle only gods know. But
one tip of one finger of the man down

touched my toe or was it my heel?
I rolled in the green meadow to see my goal
ten leagues away. Forty thousand ampitheaterans

moaned as if of one lung. It was high tragedy.
In all my dreams I see helmeted warriors
waiting, smirking. And in Thebes,

the series of old men who couldn't
find their way to where the three roads
cross, saw that play or say they did.

They smile yet. I must bear it all.
It was clear. It was meant to be. Curses.

Insecure Position

Running back
to the field, first day,
I saw the old green Ford rattle up to the front door
of the A Dorm. A worn thin, canvas sea bag
with USMC stenciled on the bottom,
rolled over the rocky walk toward me.
His war over,
his straw cowboy hat in his hand,
he wiped his forehead dry.
I noticed the beveled line of hair
as he looked about at that Ford slowly smoking away.
He was alone,
hanging clothes on his finger,
grabbing the duffel bag. In his shirt pocket
a white letter fluttered like a flag of truce
carried by a man determined to dictate terms.

Maybe 23, 24, 25. Who could tell?
Linemen maybe, linebackers, we had to have.

Big Words, Pastries

Just before a final exam in Greek Literature.
I hurriedly purchased a cream-filled pastry
from the *Amore Shop* in the plaza.
Hurrying to the exam, I slipped
it into my coat pocket. At my graffiti-profaned desk,
with my coat across my lap, I caressed my pastry,
surreptiously extracting it
when Helen joyously, gamine-like, plopped on my lap.

(A sensible man would have hung
the coat on the back of the chair, I know.
Strange what Athena, Aphrodite have us do.)

Helen felt something without doubt
odd, looked on
my mess-filled lap,
massaged her creamy butt,
misapprehended,
hurled angry imprecations at the sky.

Such words are always punished, frequently ridiculed.

For the next two years, she kept
her silence. Ten years distant
in a downward elevator
in the Worthington, we were together
with our mates. Oh the Fates!
I spoke. She did not. She turned away
like Dido. You must admire a world-class grudge.

I have contacted Guinness.

Hera taught her.

To her address, listed in the alumni bulletin,
I have mailed a box of gooey pastries
every May since that elevator meeting ten years past.
I sign "Messmaker" on a slightly altered reproduction
of Thetis with her hands on Zeus' knees,
seemingly horrified.

Reflections

The moon races along
beside my car, trying
to dart in between
the trees, bounce off
the snow and penetrate
your eyes. My heart hurries
as I strain to see
myself there too.

The Making of One More Lawyer

Watching "Demons" day after MWF day,
far more than six,
he saw them wave,
speak to other gladiators in the hall during class,
scratch themselves, amble out to the bathroom
every time they were bored,
which was once an hour.
They farted, giggled like fourth graders,
brought no notebooks, no textbooks,
but roared indignantly that they had to come to class.
Hadn't they been there?
What did he have against athaaletees?

The new M of A climbed on his desk,
shouted, "You are all in the lowest
of three non-transferable, remedial classes
at a non-selective, open-door junior college."

"Remediate, remediate," he commanded.
Spittle slid down his cheek
as they carried him out past the stadium
toward the law school.

The Price of Perfection

My father couldn't make much money
like some guys' fathers, but he could do one thing
perfectly. He could punt a football so high
it came down cold as an empty wallet.

Spirals soared up then the nose turned over.
The ball slid down softly, easy to judge
as how many dollars a bike cost.
On a blustery day, he could float it high
to catch the wind like a dream
Schwynn rolling out of your mind
as the sun shot up.

If he kicked into the wind,
he kept it low like a knuckle ball,
still spiraling, but bumping left right.
The returned doubted, misjudged,
like a kid not knowing how much cotton candy
he could eat, or the price of things.

He never missed, my father. He looked perfect
to all the guys in my world.
They would watch the ball zip to speck,
then their mouths dropped in an oblong O,
like the sun slowly, slowly setting
on the track circling the pointless field.

Grace

You taught me how to catch and to punt footballs,
to shoot pool, to play poker. When games carried songs,
smiles, I learned not to suffer long from falls.

We measured distance for all the little balls,
and big. We calculated wind, weight, pawns,
rooks, kings, though not of the great halls.

Some boys learned carpentry, then mechanics.
My sorrow-kit for their lack of time on lawns
was firmly full as bulging picnic baskets.

A boy should learn importance from his father.
I learned all there is to know about balance,
speed, thought, talk. What else to know of love or

leaping in fray could possibly be better?
You thought you never taught for fame or palace,
but in that concern you were wrong. Never bitter

about what you didn't have to give, I gathered
all that springs to birth from the many pleasured
earth. What you provided is all treasure.
To be with you was delight in full measure.

Can These Flowers Live?

Maiden Aunt Mary, always Maiden Aunt
Mary, hair as short as the heels
on her black shoes, read the bible
every hour she wasn't sewing or gardening
or dressing to go to town for church.
She read to prove she had missed nothing
but the prophets and hell's fire.
She made no bones about her perennials
and planted way up there, in the middle
of the north pasture, her purple violets
and other flowers no one has names
for now. They are there, still defying
cash crops, fleshing out each year
and blessing, always blessing,
Momma's grave and Poppa's.
Cars stop and men take off their hats,
then mop their brows while women
take pictures, preserving forever
the acres of purple flowers
in the middle of cotton,
replanted year after year.

Forecast

(Mark 4:26-29)

The sky is full threat; the wind billows
black clouds from the mountains.
The calving heifers twitch tails
in the stable, ignored by horses
and cats who live by milk, mice.
My son and I scan the valley for our collie,
but, pursuing some heavenly scent
he is far from the electricity that runs off,
guilty. By fire and flashlight I read
of the prodigal. At the door during lightning
strokes we hear our dog, whimpering.
My son pulls the wet, smelly beast in, hugs
him to a place by the fire, covers dirty
matted hair with a good towel as I turn
to the parable of the seed sown.

Goodness Knows

She went her way. She'll find me later,
I thought. I walked straight as virtue
south with my almost useless .410 breached under my arm.
The deep meadow grass
waved me along with the northerly
breeze. Thinking to check the west fence,
I turned right
for a hundred yards. Finding little
of value hiding in holes,
I followed my path
back to the original
rut.

On briefly south
then seeing a cross
through the narrow creek,
I came back,
trekked
east through the gushing water,
then up
the hill to sit, watch the sun
fall.

My collie came running
far below me
following
my scent. She was perfect:
south, west, then east to the pure water
where she lost me. She followed

the same route over and over
believing
she could find me.
I waved my crooked scepter,
but she could not see me.

Content,
I watch her
invoke blessing after blessing.

Traces

In Memoriam C.H.R. 1920-1986

As you pulled the old horse or mule drawn plow
from its nails on the barn wall, you turned to me,
but looked beyond and forgot your usual flow
about your place in the city's world, the fees
you earned. The life you lifted from the rich
soil again became a part of you.
You laughed at your slow-time pace behind big
wooden hames and crusty traces that knew
the tasks long dropped from the new-day thoughts.
We pointed to the lake with the fishing rod
that witched us to the water. We lifted, not bought,
turned-up worms protruding from soft sods
of almost clay with a tenacious hold
on your homesick view of place where I grow old.

Theories of Child Rearing

in Memoriam L.M.R. 1928-1998

Mother's calm becalmed my wayward accusers.
Her cool demeanor, not always her behavior,
sent a brisk, tidy response to the angry churchmen.
Uncoiling, like Thetis from the water,
she said, "I learn his wants. If it's no sin,
I get it for him." Islands of stranded pain,
like marooned seamen signaling in vain,
their prelatical faces fell in clerical splatter.
They wavered beside the baptism font, defeated.
Indolent as lazy waves sweeping seaward
I steered her from their dried up clatter.
At the altar rail, she kneeled and whispered:
"Thank you, Son. You remind me of your father.
He was an iconoclast and no good either."

Elegy for a Former Teacher

A screech of tires
in a minor key
and she was gone.

She had been
a music teacher,
a good-looking woman
who taught method
and knew rhythm.

I remember her swaying
to her beat,
crescendo after crescendo.

Young eighth notes arranged
themselves on the sheet
music just for her.
She played them fast.

A drunken boy in his father's car
the paper said.
Nothing else of note.

Veritas Liberabit Vos

When one of the brothers
was pinned, my fraternity
serenaded her sorority.
I noted carefree singing
of love songs. I thought we lied
to one another, to one other.

Our chords
struck sympathetic overtones in tower bells.

God sent a seraphim
to hymn angelic harmony
for my song.
Her golden, layered hair
flowed about my throat
strangling dissonant sounds.

She was more luscious than celestial wine,
softer than suspicions,
more desirable than the grail,
than the cloistered letter jacket
a preppie had to be cool to wear.

The coat clung to her
one ephemeral night, covering then undoing
doubts
with crescendos.

Twenty years later the hallowed coat
is as new and attractive as original sin.
Sometimes I feverishly stick my nose
between buttons, catch a whiff
of the old stupefying incense,
rub my face in Angel dust
until her halo glows. An infinity
later, in the shower, I sing timeless tunes.

Couchant Bryant, Headmaster

In his teak cafetorium, he presided.
In making announcements, about school
functions or bodily ones, his thighs collided,
never knees. Under the thin-legged table,
we watched his flesh flap and flop about
like dolphins playing beside an angled bow.

His eyes were never bigger than his brunch,
and he stuffed all his fold-filled face could crunch
into his famous gut. Three hundred pounds,
excluding chins, would arise. Pink jowls sunk around
a lipless mouth. His booming voice would bellow
imperious commands for silence. Shushing sounds
rose and slid beneath the ripples and flow
of flesh.
       Boys bulged their eyes, sucked air deep in
with round-lipped awe. Couchant kept syllables trim.

The Trophy Room

We hunted in the trophy room
around the pool table and bar.
"Bring on The High Hard Ones,"
was written in thick, hard foam
with sequins in it and was forever stuck
on a mirror, underneath
a drawing of an oversized baseball bat.
Animal heads, with necks,
vied for space on every wall,
each erect
and standing out.
Betty, Rhonda, Louis and I turned on
darkness to play Hide and Seek. We crawled
the woods of furniture, bumping legs
of stuffed chairs, hard tables,
and searched with glassy eyes.

The original touch
was best.
After the first impression,
we had to identify the prey
by shoulders, hair, or face.
Unmade
rules but understood.

Come summer
I killed my first deer.

Hide and Seek
gave the three of us
a better feel
for life
I could not understand
for years.

Whispers

Joannie Kate sang in the choir
because I did. Everyone knew.
She was tall, slim, wore glasses
and had an hour-glass figure
below a face as long as six o'clock.
On choir trips after dark
she put herself in my hands.
Late hours we met in the bus barn
where she would whisper my name.

In the light of days, I knew
no time for her, but the dark
of the moon heard her breath
upon me, as I drifted like sand
to her, this first girl who wanted me.

Later, she gracefully directed
singers of timeless music
at the high school, married a mortician, ·
and died of breast cancer.
Breath-filled arpeggios from sibilant
youths protected her, or so I thought.

When she slid beyond sound,
beyond measured beats,
I sent a requiem mass
of wavering bouquets—
perennials—
to the bus barn.

Always in my view
one violet lies
by the bus barn wall
with light moth wing shadows
fanning its petals.

The sun stands still for her;
I hear her breathe my name
when the wind, moon rise.

The Ring of Kappa Alpha Order

for DB

Though I would push the frat away, it holds
and clings, until scars remain embedded in
my thoughts, refusing to grow decrepit, just old.
The wonder-grasp on me has grown so strong
that my spotted hand has aged around a pen,
scratching for reasons to explain a claim long
endured, deep throughout my psyche within
a shining, infinite ring of ten carat gold.
Why should I write? No reason but peace from art—
a mere sleight of hand, designed to confound
a belief that brotherhood could start
on lackbrain theories of eternal friends.
Among a tribe of erudites, the shaman's
duties are thought to be the will of the clan.

The Perfect Mate

You can be anything but Roseanne Barr
or maybe Momma Cass.
I'd like you to be tall, lean, blonde—
a sort of Princess Grace,
but Audrey Hepburn would be nice.

Don't be impressed by the rich.
Read books, not best sellers.
Understand *The Bridges of Madison County,*
The English Patient are baaad.

No jewels, no perfume, especially no earrings,
no fingernail polish. Be bored by sports.
Love country, classical music.
A glass of wine at the end of some good days is nice.
Walk two miles a day. Be afraid I might die.
Let me calm you. Notice no insults.
Feel sorry for those who hurt,
especially those who hurt you. Love our children
beyond measure. Never watch Jerry Springer.

If you have these ways or don't have them,
understand
you cannot get away from me.
Divorce me,
and I will move in next door to you.
I don't care
if you get to be as fat as Roseanne,
don't act like her. I know you

won't. I'll never become John Goodman.
I promise. I can't be Cary Grant.
I'm more like Groucho,
but I'll be a sweet Groucho for you.

Burning

Your neighbors never know
you're a poet. Your parents worry,
your children count their toes, embarrassed.

At the family reunion, Uncle Orville,
the rich one with the young, pretty wife,
laughs at your parents, ignores your children,
talks, brags about his deals not too slyly.

When the conversation turns
from him in white hot sun he proclaims:
"A poet! by God, how's he make a living?"

Mother pales, Father reddens, stammers, "Teaching."
Miriam, the pretty young wife, smiles,
with her thighs, bends, brushes a fly off her narrow ankle,
offers me a breast.

Her eyes are a picnic. She asks me for something to read,
says she loves what I do. She doesn't understand much,
but Uncle Orville, turning from pale to glaring red, does.

Genesis

From nowhere known
it arrives. You try to coax it
to come to you; you feed it.

You give up, try to leave it
but like a puppy,
it comes after you
and follows you around
and around, liking the game.

Or sometimes you throw
it about in some recently lit
corner of your mind
that could blacken
suddenly like a tennis court
somebody else put
the quarters in for.

It could hit you
just after black strikes.
Maybe you'll crawl in the dark
hoping to find it
before you hate yourself
for losing it, for giving up.

Honor

My father was the point of the triangle
as I was flanked by uncles. Mother was distant,
sobbing slightly, out of sight behind the barn.
Honor was father's word, and I took
my usual bracing stance when he used it.
He looked into my eyes. Uncles were quiet
as ex-marines on parade. He put too much money
into my hand: "Go to your war, if you must,
but come home with your shield or without it."

The sun and moon have circled and hidden
each other many times since that day.
I have seen my ring of friends broken
in flames, had my luck, but I have never
been richer than that glaring moment
when mother's eyes were red as cinders.

Second Tour

When ten or so, he went to high school football practices.
It was a long way from their place to town,
to the football field. His Dad took
the car to the city, to work. The son never
had a bike. How did he get there or home?

The stands were often not full.
The important men were always together.
They asked about his father, pointed proudly
to the field. When he played, Charley Eubanks
of *Eubanks and Hern* gave him a pair of shoes.
In the drug store, he had his own cup
with his name on it. It was sometimes empty.

He came home from college one weekend.
The small bus station was full.
His Dad told him people at church asked about him.

Five years after college he came home
for a good time, for good.
Mrs. Jefferson, widow of the banker, nodded.
I.B. Cupp, who owned the newspaper, waved
from across the street.
At church, polite, cordial smiles.

He looked at high school, college letter jackets,
polished his shoes, pinned ribbons back on,
hugged, kissed his red-eyed mother,
shook his pale father's spotted hand,

hugged him too. His Dad drove him
to an early, empty plane
back to San Diego.
He felt lost going through Pendleton's main gate,
wondered: how did I get here?

Cosmic

After five years a Marine, three years
between visits, he appears to his family:
visitation by a stranger in a well-lighted room.
Back slaps, like shocking thunder,
boom in his ears while black eyes
in white faces eyes, eyes he can see himself in,
try to take him in.
He slips back to dark nights
where brothers from a larger family
looked up at white stars, too many
to count, at slivers of light
flickering off never fully known.

In Cisco, Texas

Here, no one comes to visit
to see the sights. In San Francisco,
well scrubbed guests arrived at the door,
bags in hand, sheepish smiles
on their faces, with plans to scamper
in well known directions. Fewer friends
arrive now, but those who come
have no plans, their hands reach
for the dog's head. They see sheep,
mesquite, scrub oak, the smile
on my face, and stars meandering
to nowhere known.

The Mayor

Would you be the Mayor
of Cisco, Tx—a town full
of Rottweilers and Pit Bulls
with nothing to guard? You know
the word moribund? Cisco
is mostabund. A bad joke,
Cisco, but the Mayor—
what is he to do? Nights he hears
Ft. Worth/ El Paso pulsing by
on the interstate. He sees the town,
his florist shop, decaying.
Wal-Mart snubs him.
No McDonald's, and a tornado
brushed away the Diary Queen
like broken glass in a dust pan.
No plans to rebuild.
The street lights dim.

Looking Deep

Occasionally, when trotting out
to far away work across the creek,
Johnny and I see fish. They are
different sizes and shapes, but like old
men and ladies at church they all look
much the same. One comes up
to stare then returns to his group
bubbling about something deep.
Another breaks away, leaves the protection
of his kind and comes to register
astonishment. With only a quick look
through the sometimes clear water,
he returns to a safe dark place
to nod in agreement with friends
about things above them all.
Johnny, my friend, sits on his roan,
and says that it is a seasonal thing
that the fish are going somewhere.
His insights are good enough for me.
The world is full of secrets.

Making the Grade

Living on a flat land ranch
and teaching in a college on a hill
is a simple life. Six miles
from the college, I sequester myself
on my principality, but the worlds
are connected. Occasionally the radio
and tv tell me about that other world—
schedules and such. At night
Fred and Ginger sometimes tap
out messages about up-hill battles.

From my place, I can see the highway
weaving its way up the hills,
connecting the quilt of country
to the college where I am mastered,
often. Each morning I eye my gate

reluctantly, pierce reality and draw
myself toward a tapestry of minds seemingly
interested only in things as simple as A B C.

First Light

Saddling my horse in the early morning
dark, I try to remember how many high-headed
colts have become heavy, resigned old horses
under my saddles. How many times have I
stood at the gate feeling for the latch
fearing a snake might be near? Have I
known where dangers lay? Trotting
out further in the black, I wonder
if my father had such thoughts
on this road. How many times will my sons
wait for the amber glow of morning on this way?
When I see the outline of cow and calf
in the beginning light, I put aside
these thoughts one more time.

The Middle

About halfway to the pens
across the creek
I tell Johnny
that after four days
working cattle
my hands are blistered
my back sore
and if I flank
one more calf
that throws its head
back into my knee
I'll be too stove up
to mount my green-broke filly
for the ride back to the barn.

He listens to the distant windmill whir
spits brown tobacco juice
on the green cactus
we can never be rid of
and says, "You're at the cowboy
in-between age—too old to outwork
and outrope the kids
but too young
to enter
the oldtimer ropings."

I refuse to smile
and hide my dreams
like the raw flesh
under my gloves.

Longevity

Uncle Emmit died of a mad dog bite
at age nineteen. Fifty-year-old Uncle Fred
from a horse who fell backward and drove
a saddle horn through his chest. Uncle
Bob from a heart attack at age forty-two.
Uncle Wade was attacked by his heart
unto death at age fifty-nine. Cousin Ralph
lasted until he was forty-five—heart too.
I'm ahead of the game and feel like a winner,
but cousin Ike, who finished high school,
said he thought there was no point
in my having earned a doctorate if I had to die
too. I nodded slowly and sipped cautiously
another glass of cousin Ralph's homemade wine.

On Calf Roping

The first thing to do
after your filly is warm
is check your equipment.
Tighten your cinch.
When the calf darts right then left
and all your weight shifts,
things better hold.
Tighten the flank strap.
She could get hurt
in the withers.
Don't forget the skid pads.
A horse burned
skidding
won't stop for you again.
Tighten your rope hard
to the horn that sticks up
in front of you.
Build your loop;
put the piggin string in your mouth.
Get her in the roping box easy,
back her till she touches.
Now wait.
The calf must look forward.
Your horse must relax.
The chute opens;
you're THRUST in the arena.
This is the excitement,
the brief moment
you can almost remember.

44

The calf might run hard
for the back end
or maybe run dirty
darting left right.
Stay close.
EXPLODE
your loop.
Run down the rope,
tie.
You walk back
to your horse,
exhausted, satisfied.

A Farewell Party

For Johnny

I rode by your house today
the first time since.
The gate was open and a bull
calf was on the porch.
Something sucked the tail
of your checkered curtain
out of a broken window.
It waved me away, waved good-bye.
I turned to leave, but then I
remembered the way you would
begin to hum some tuneless song,
pull your hat far down
on your head and how your eyes
lit up when you began to build
your loop. I came back,
eased the sorrel you liked
through the gate, and chased
the motly-faced intruder
into the already sagging
fence, then roped and dragged
the arrogant black beast back
where he belonged. I smiled
thinking of your approval
then laughed and laughed
until my vision blurred.
I turned the sorrel loose
to feed on cactus flowers
and tried to watch
as the sun slid off somewhere.

Unplanned Obsolescing

In late fall when a man reaches
for the lawnmower in his garage,
he grasps a tilted baseball bat
and breathes faster,
hoping for a high hard one.

The pipes under his leaking sink
squeal a little like the lithe lady VP
who won't touch messy Xerox parts.

When a middle management man
leaves his wife
every morning,
he loves a minute
with a creamy-skinned secretary
generously massaging the coffee machine
as she pours rich, hot, striking substance
into his steamy cup.

October Song

Young bosoms bursting
through thin, loose-weave blouses,
tan legs beneath black shorts,
bare bellies flat out
make a man
whimper, mourn cool,
love summer.

Bare legs bicycling
through Spring
pump warmth
even into Fall.

Her red lips round
to greet ground ice.
She scoops her eyes
up at me and sucks
red juice into the corners
of her delicious mouth.

Reunion

Barbara was pure
redhead
whose vision burned
in our brains
until we could see
ourselves
in flaming
green eyes.

She glistened, burnished:
a vessel for any price.

She glared through us
made us commit,

married a hero,
saw him unfaithful,
served him
children.

Remorseful, insightful,
we returned
to where wives waited,
brushing flies away,
showing pictures
of grandchildren
with brown, black, golden hair
staring at us
with impenetrable eyes.

Who Will Stop Him?

In a world of burgeoning MBAs
who will listen to the stories of Tudors, Stewarts,
contending for gold long sunk, already spent?

Quaint, unimportant religions intruding on bankers,
Kings? Impossible.

Who will call him Dr.?

Megabytes, gigahertz, trolls, elves,
Does he believe in such things?
He didn't cave to Polyphemus. Took that in.

Can a man of 65 years
learn to be relevant in a business world—
a man sunk
forty years deep in thought?
How can he retire?
How in a sound-bitten punditocracy
can Cokie Roberts, Sam Donaldson
explain old Mithridates
sampling all the earth's killing store?

Don't they know they need him?
Who will tell them?

December

Today I look bleakly out of a mirror
filled with Bosse's death,
reflect on George's emphysema,
Halton's forty-percent heart, Bill's less.
Lawrence caught Lou Gehrig's
slow, drowning death. I see
myself alone too long. Laid out is the plan.

Come look in the deep, my father calls.
I cannot run down to the dock
to sail in a rudderless skiff.
My sons stare at frosty breath
drifting over hoary caps.

Does the lighthouse beckon wind,
the tree call lightning?

Revisited

My maiden aunt Mary came to visit
for a whole month every summer.
She always told the same stories
about how young Jeffery took
her for rides on these same ranch roads
in his 1937 Ford every Sunday
and how he had wanted her
to marry him, but he was killed
in the war. She said nothing
was very nice after that. The traffic
on the highway grew too loud,
and the April roses stopped
smelling so sweet. No romance, she said.

Now I visit her in Dallas once
a month. She says her room
is never warm; the "Villa" reeks
of rubbing alcohol, and the other
residents complain about her blaring TV.
Then she falls asleep while telling me
what has happened this last month
to the various villains, heroes, doctors
and nurses who, between commercials,
come to visit her every day.

Only Thoughts Return to the Same True Places

We told the same old stories all week
and laughed at the same places
in the narratives where we always did.
Tonight, we lie in four different beds
all bound to journey in different
directions while the world travels
no known path. The moon lights
my wife for a few minutes, then shifts
its focus searching. She turns, sleeping,
dreaming of her sons laughing, playing.
Alarm sounds and vacation ends.
She fails to notice the moon receding,
the slight rising of the sun. The wind
pushes the heavy heads of grain toward
us. Horses in the corral calmly crowd
one another, brushing away annoyance
coming in with the morning heat. Sons
ready to leave with their true wives.

Childish

to Martin

A stoop-shouldered English professor
forced a senior out of registration,
made him go back about three hours
in the process because the student's trial study schedule
was not "neat." It was barely legible,
but such schedules are for the student only.
The student seethed.

One year later the new graduate student
was whistling his way to class
in a crowded hallway. The professor
came out of his office, remembered something,
set a leather briefcase with his brassy initials on it
by the open door to his office.
A pretty sophomore girl in a red dress
followed him in and shut the door.
The usually timid student
picked up the case confidently,
realizing that with every step he was risking a life sentence
in a gas station or selling encyclopedias.
He hurried out the front entrance, delicately balanced
the case on the narrow concrete rail by the steps. Now
thirty years later, almost at retirement age,
he is still pleased and unpenitant.

Destination

for B S

A man appears at her window,
watching her glancing up occasionally
from magazines pictures of autumn scenes.
Light moth shadows fan
gentle, quick movements of darkness
on her face as she turns and turns
again with the music he can faintly
hear, but he can't dance nimbly
because he cannot remember her
face when he steps back in swirls
of snow to float in music that grows
softer as he dances. He stops,
forgetting the music, the moment.

The woman imagines the man outside
her window, dancing.
She shifts her position, looks out
at the movement as he steps back in snow,
leaving only a brief print.

In her study there is no door;
in snow he turns from her.

In his dreams she follows him
through a green forest.
She does not raise her eyes.

Friday Afternoon

That soul of honor, Robert E. Lee, is astride
his Traveler in the park. My empty eyes,
captured by his, absorbed his hours
while I was waiting for the Lady writer
from New York from long ago. She found life
halting in a conventional way and was in town
till noon Sunday. We stood where we lay
thirty years before and talked of old knights.
Nothing comes from such talk, bare talk.
The general's shadow didn't fall as the day
leaned toward a cloudy night. Then I was alone
and level headed, thinking about time, sands,
dust, old visages. I stretched no boundaries
to put my hand on a knee, cold and bronze.

Delivered

Tumbleweeds cover the fence
outside this west Texas motel.
They have come storming in
with the sand. We look out
from our room to a world
dark as nature. This night
stolen ftom another world
holds what the wind delivered.

Consecrated

My eyes cannot persuade me that you are old.
After some forty years apart we close
Again to some state within where we behold
Young selves, a pretty, yet vain view. No pose
For one another holds as new. We are
Not young, but old in worlds by love entranced,
Where we along our path see no true bar
To love's own way. Our vision thus enhanced
By past love's glow, we only dimly see
That which we would become from our desire.
The magic holds and we forget, then flee
The forces forged by love's second strong fire.
My eyes shall not persuade me you are old;
No truth intrudes. Desire and love are bold.

Incalculable

Is virtue your faith? And me, is love my sin?
Because I love and cannot help myself,
Must I conclude the fault is deep within
My genes? Or can I blame some capricious elf?
But you, are you so certain you're on the path
Of God's own plan that you can throw us away?
You calculate your answers in God's math,
But are numbers known—insight by damned old clay?
Not many days are left for us to seize,
But there is no doubt for any: the best is yet
Not free: we'll pay. Don't care if we displease
The fates; the infinite fine scheme is set
Per diem. Discount the charges for fustion fun,
And know our journey goes beyond the sun.

In pace requiescat

To my sons

You almost never remembered birthdays, so
Try hard to mark and notice the annual day
Of my death. You could ring bells, sound sirens, and go
About with short faces. Be sure to pay
The priest again and please joyfully embrace
My mistress who gave herself with hope—
A cheerful giver. Wipe tears from her wrong face
And if you should pass by the place the Pope
Would put his emissary, please pray for her
Without the woeful sorriest of sounds:
The organ that booms and blows to warn, a burr
Within the ear of man that scares and pounds
The message home: another sinner's gone.
When you reflect on my request, don't moan.

Vineyards

When strolling through arbors,
choosing poems to intoxicate you,
luxurious good taste demands
I select certain reddish vines.

Your shimmering petals,
show succulence.
I desire to swallow you
like vivid heady lines.

Entranced

I strapped golden time
on your wrist, forced
a shimmering cross between your breasts,
wrapped your long slender finger
with gold.

Weighted, you could not betray
your winsome stance,
but sway gently,
chime softly to my soul.

Your lulling music, dance
gives me power
to fend off dragon fire,
protect our poem bower.

Will

Grandfather William was lean as a whip.
He wore vested suits,
coat buttoned to the top.
A great gray mustache hid an upper lip I never saw.

He never bent in the saddle,
not at a gallop,
not going through brush.
His hat never blew off.

He was eighty-one
when I rode to his house to see him
at the hitching post
beside a banging kitchen door,
struggling to lift his heavy saddle
to the back of a big bay horse.

His arms were shaking as he held the saddle
pinned between his chest and the bay.

He looked at me with moist eyes,
dropped the saddle in the dust.

He looked at the bay, shifted his blue eyes to my face.
"I never rode a horse 'cept I saddled it."
He looked at the empty house
where my father was born.

"I'd have to stay here, wouldn't I?"

"Yes, Grandpa, you would," I said,
reaching for the saddle,
old and cracked at his feet.

The Last Supper

After the last supper
at the last resort
before your vacation
ends, pat your wife
on the knee, over-tip
your waiter, hug
the cashier, kiss
the doorman, and laugh
all the way home.

Closing Time

When the snow lifts off of roofs in silver swirls,
the wind dominates trees
that bend
in supplication till their roots show.
Birds swell,
turn tail to the wind,
fight for balance.

Travelers hesitate
just inside doors,
grab at the remaining warmth like women
covering their knees
as if their lives
depend on virtue.

The day does not hover
even a moment
before the sky blackens. A pale passenger
slides by in a car, his face frosting the window
as the wind gathers its own;
birds, pushed,
try to rise above the sweepings of white dust,
lose their way.

Visitors, reluctant at day's end,
fly through a door
they thought to slip open, peep through
while waiting for a better time.

Too Much Death

Boys, sons mine, I want "Lil Darling"
by the Diamonds PLAYED LOUD.
I want my middle finger raised
from the coffin, pointing up. Hire
an out of work actor to hit the Priest
in the face with a pie. Fill
the coffin with rocks and my main
remains. As for the bearers of pall,

                      Find

a list on me of women
who will be surprised
to have been called on.   Hope
they stumble, fall and curse
in mud to the final
swear word.   Pray
for rain, umbrella-ripping wind.
Hire a driver who loses   His way
to the cemetery.   Turn to Him
to go back toward
the people in the car line. Wave
vigorously. You may   Shed
a polite tear or two from laughter,
but remember much mourning is   Sin.

When It's Time

*The only way to keep your health
is to eat what you don't want,
drink what you don't like, and
do what you'd rather not.*
　　　　　　—Mark Twain, *Puddin'head Wilson*

When it's time to go
I want to know
so I can grab a breath
in an oak-floored pool hall
and wait for death
with a can of Skoal
and a case of Lone Star longneckers
while lucky old men play checkers.

Beck's Dead, Damn 2000

Not only God
knows the number of hairs on Beck's head.
Six wispy long, gray strands
fold on two, thin, yellowish satin pillows.

Then

golden memories fly like thick, black curls,
convoluted by rolled-down car-window wind,
strong as the hot-air ins and outs of your stories.

With Melba Jean caressing,
untangling your twisted, curly locks
before school in the famous "Four-Stroke"
47 Chevy, I was ready to believe
anything you said about dark doings.
Impressionistic leather backseat covers
rose from indention's depressed witness
to hint what you un-reluctantly confirmed—
triumphs lifted like exploding piston heads.

Beck buddy, when I slide in again
where you are, in the back seat,
I want some good tales.

In any heaven worth having,
Melba Jean is making you
purr like some big black furry
cat in her lap. For my prayers
and pounds of candles,
you fix me up
with the straight scoop, deal?

Swell.
Your stories make time zip by
like a souped-up Chevy heading for the drive-in.

An Annual Solution

Never raised his hand or voice to me
and when a man doesn't say much, you tend
to listen. My father would pull me aside
and force instruction on me like dictation.
Damned if he didn't feel compelled to help
nature. When he decided winter was over,
no matter the calendar, selection was made
and any animal who was shaggy or too close
was sheared. Horses had to look good for father—
a trader. They stood, fetlock deep, in shorn
hair and would crowd one against the other,
hiding, warding off shame and cold.
I remember them, always, like grainy black
and white film of Jews, naked, hairless,
covering private parts with their hands
as they were shot. Some last indignity,
herded together, hairless. I pulled
my Stetson down snug, never doubting
father's final solution.

Empty Nest New Year

He hears "Daddy " in the wind.
His head whips around.
The car stops at *Athletic Supply.*
He fondles gloves, balls.
Remembers high ones and low.

Home, he walks out to stare at the black mare,
wondering when she foals who will know?
When will excitement occur?
Young city men have little time.

Baseball bats stand in the corner.
Mother cooks without input, interest.
A tasteless dinner eaten slowly by a retired rancher,
waiting for the phone. He reads sports, remembers
exciting Decembers,
talking about Johnny Unitas,
watching Tommy Nobis.

Father's Perfect Funeral

My goodness, my father would have enjoyed
his funeral. The driver on the road to salvation
in a stretched-out car lost his way.
Endless cars, some out of sight behind us,
turned into the same driveway to go back
in our search for the true church.
We met those who had followed,
waved vigorously, signaled
like a base coach
sending messages about the road
to heaven. A serpentining row of followers
docilely turning-in, backing out
of the same pathway, continued a doubt-filled journey.
Mother shed laughter like memories.
The driver struggled. There was no stopping
for him. Those waiting at the church
looked down, thinking the earth might open,
pull them in. Those arriving smiled at the earth,
knowing it held nothing of consequence.

What Comes of Home Burial

I must ride by sometimes.
I try not to look at the land.
It's the sky that blankets all.
A little land that one becomes
is too small. I imagine mother, father
down there. I hear them calling me
to come to them. Their voices louder,
stronger than the day father urged me
to step from the high board
at the club pool.

From even a slight distance above,
the tops of tombs
must seem like cornices of windows
seen from the street. The fence around Momma, Poppa,
Aunt Mary, what for?
The dead come closer each trip to the south pasture.
I beg their blurred faces: let me pass.

The ways of dying are numerous as the ways of living.
I fear them all.
Poppa, the day of your death
was dark but with pinholes of light
like streamers of bright ribbons
to show the way.

Send some sign, a sacrament, a creed,
a myth, a doctrine, some kind message for your inheritor,
passing by your fence, looking above your window,
who has no understanding.

Tender Mercy

Almighty God
to whom all hearts are open,
I know Thee.

You desire for me to know
beams that hold,
fires that warm,
water that purifies,
has strength to crush,
power to burn,
ability to extinguish.
No secrets are hid.

Cleanse my heart. I am
creation,
not extension.
There could be
no pleasure without me.
Your image I am.
I imperfectly love Thee.

The Border

When a person has nothing more to say,
or worse, nothing more to think,
he should drive far unto the brink
of thought, say . . . Oklahoma.

Motor through familiar lands
and see the comfortable
farms and well developed plans.
Note a warping red gable
and high cloud-filled unending skies.
Pass through flat lands until you see
the end—an old state with no guard.
Then turn to home and tell no lies
about an easy, relaxing journey,
but hold the vision in high regard.